PAGES YET TO TURN

JAGDISH GURJAR

To every dreamer standing at the edge of a decision.

To every tired heart who still finds the courage to believe.

To everyone who dared to believe that they were one step away from changing their life.

To those who stumble but stand up again.

To those who walk quietly when no one is cheering.

To those who know deep down that giving up is not an option.

This book is for you.

Contents

Foreword

We often wait for the perfect time to begin.
We believe success is meant for the gifted, for the lucky, for the extraordinary.

But the truth is simple.
Success belongs to those who dare to take the next step — even when it's hard, even when it's uncertain, even when it feels small.

The difference between a dreamer and a doer is not talent, but action.
It is not destiny, but decision.

Every great story begins with a single step forward.
Not a leap. Not a miracle.
Just one step.

This book is not about massive overnight victories.
It's about the quiet, powerful decision to move forward when everything inside you says to stay still.

I am not speaking to you as someone who has conquered it all, but as someone who believes that no matter where you are, you are always one step away from transforming your life.

This book is a conversation, not a lecture.
It is my heart to yours.

Let's begin —
Let's walk together.
— Jagdish Gurjar

Preface

There's a moment in life when we realize that change is not something that happens overnight, or by accident.
It happens because of conscious choices, tiny actions, and invisible efforts.
When I started working toward my own goals, I often felt overwhelmed.
Dreams seemed huge.
Failures felt permanent.
Success looked reserved for the lucky or the rich or the extraordinary.
But as I kept walking — step by step —
I understood something that changed my life forever:
The distance between where you are and where you want to be is just one step.
One decision.
One risk.
One conversation.
One act of faith.
You don't need a perfect plan to start.
You don't need approval from the world.
You don't even need to be ready.
You just need to move.
One step forward.
This book is born out of my belief that anyone — no matter where they begin — can create a life of meaning, courage, and fulfillment if they stop waiting for the perfect moment and start stepping toward it.
Each page you are about to read is written for you — the dreamer, the fighter, the believer — who knows deep inside that life can be more.
You are closer than you think.
You are one step away.
Let's begin.

Acknowledgements

Writing this book has been a journey of discovery, not just into the world of success, but into myself.

First and foremost, I want to thank my family, who have always believed in me even when I doubted myself.
Your patience, support, and silent prayers have carried me farther than words can express.

To the mentors I've never met — the teachers, speakers, dreamers whose words fueled my early steps — thank you.
Your courage to share your journeys gave me the courage to share mine.

To every friend who stood by me quietly, who understood my silences, who never judged the days I disappeared into work and dreams — I see you, and I am grateful for you.

To the readers holding this book in their hands:
Thank you for trusting me with your time, your attention, and your dreams.
I do not take it lightly.

Finally, to the younger version of myself — the boy who was scared but moved forward anyway — this book is your victory.
Thank you for not giving up when it would have been easier to quit.

This is not the end of a journey, but just another step forward.
And I am honored to be walking this path together with you.

ACKNOWLEDGEMENTS

Prologue

You probably don't realize it yet, but you're standing at the edge of
something extraordinary.

It doesn't feel like it.

Maybe you're tired.

Maybe you're unsure.

Maybe your past still echoes too loudly, and your future feels like a fog you
can't see through.

That's how every journey starts —

not with trumpets or certainty,

but with fear, hope, and a tiny voice inside whispering:

"Maybe... just maybe... I can do this."

The world won't always see your potential.

Sometimes even you won't.

You'll doubt. You'll delay. You'll dream, then freeze.

But here's the truth:

You are never as stuck as you feel.

You are never as far as you fear.

You are always one step away —

One step away from a breakthrough.

One step away from rebuilding.

One step away from beginning the life you secretly want.

This book is not about running marathons in a day.

It's about learning to take one more step —

and realizing that every small step you take is rewriting your destiny.

If you've picked up this book,

you're already braver than you think.

You've already taken the first step.

Now let's take the next one — together.

CHAPTER ONE

The First Step

There's a moment in every person's life when everything could change —

and that moment often looks small from the outside.

It's not winning a lottery.

It's not meeting a billionaire mentor.

It's not a dramatic TV moment that announces, "Today, your life will change."

It's something far simpler —

You wake up one day and decide to take **one step.**

One gym session.

One call made.

One idea written down.

One risk taken.

One small victory — even if no one notices.

And inside that first, quiet, invisible move,
something extraordinary is happening:
You are changing your own story.

The Myth of the Giant Leap

We are taught to admire giant leaps —
The athlete who wins gold overnight.
The startup that becomes a billion-dollar company instantly.
The actor who "suddenly" becomes a star.
But real change rarely happens with one big dramatic jump.
It's built through **small, deliberate, consistent steps —**
in silence, in difficulty, when no one is watching.
One step might not look impressive.
It might feel too small to matter.
But if you take one step today — and another tomorrow —
soon, you are no longer the same person.
You are no longer standing at the starting line.
You are moving, growing, becoming.

Courage Is Smaller Than You Think

We imagine courage looks like standing on a battlefield or speaking to a crowd of thousands.
But often, courage is much quieter:

- It's choosing to get out of bed when your heart is heavy.
- It's writing the first sentence of a dream project even if no one may read it.
- It's applying for a job even after being rejected ten times.
- It's forgiving yourself for the past and trying again today.

The first step doesn't require you to be fearless.
It only requires you to be **willing**.

Movement Creates Momentum

You don't have to figure everything out today.
You don't have to solve all your problems at once.
    You just have to start.
    Movement creates momentum.
Momentum changes your emotions.
Emotions fuel better actions.
Actions create new results.
Results build new beliefs.
    It's a cycle — and it all begins with the first step.

The Hardest Step Is Often the Smallest

The first workout after years of laziness is the hardest.
The first honest conversation after months of hiding is the hardest.
The first attempt after failures is the hardest.
    Why?
    Because starting challenges your self-doubt.
It demands you to leave your comfort zone.
It threatens your fears of rejection, embarrassment, and failure.
    But once you take that step, you realize —
It was never as impossible as you feared.
    The chain of failure you thought was unbreakable snaps instantly with a
single act of courage.

You Already Know Your First Step

As you read these words, you already know what your "first step" is.
It's been whispering to you for days, months, maybe years.
    You don't need another motivational speech.
You don't need permission.
You don't need a perfect plan.
    You already know.
    Now, trust yourself enough to move.

One Step Today, Not Tomorrow

Not next Monday.
Not when you "feel ready."

Not after the perfect circumstances appear.

Today.

Today is the only day you can control.

Today is the only battlefield where success is fought and won.

Take one step today — however small, however scared you feel.

And then tomorrow, take one more.

And the day after that, another.

This is how empires are built.

This is how lives are changed.

This is how you become unstoppable.

CHAPTER TWO

The Distance That Isn't Real

We have been conditioned to believe that dreams are distant —
that success is sitting somewhere across oceans and mountains,
while we stand helpless at the shore.

But that's a lie.

The truth is,

the distance is an illusion.

You are closer to your dreams than you think.
Closer than you feel.
Closer than you dare to believe.

The problem is not the size of the dream —
the problem is the way you measure distance.

You see, dreams are not measured in kilometers, years, or bank balances.
They are measured in actions.
Every action you take pulls the dream closer.
Every excuse you make pushes it further.

Dreams Look Far When You Stand Still

Imagine standing at the bottom of a staircase.
If you freeze and stare at the top, it looks impossibly high.
You feel small, weak, discouraged.
But the moment you lift your foot and climb the first step,
the journey transforms.
Suddenly, it's not a mountain —
it's just a series of small steps.
The same is true with any dream:
starting shrinks the fear.
movement kills the illusion.
When you stay still, problems magnify.
When you move, solutions appear.

Belief is the Bridge

Most people never begin,
because they believe the destination is unreachable.
But belief is the bridge between you and your dream.
If you believe it's possible, you find ways.
If you believe it's impossible, you find excuses.
Belief doesn't make the work easier —
but it makes it **possible**.
It transforms overwhelming into achievable.
It turns someday into today.

No One is Born at the Top

Look closely at anyone you admire:
The bestselling author once wrote stories no one read.
The entrepreneur once sold a product no one bought.
The artist once painted in a room where no one clapped.

The athlete once trained when no one was watching.
They were not born standing on stages.
They climbed there,
one invisible, thankless, silent step at a time.
They faced the same doubts, fears, rejections you feel.
But they understood something:
Standing still guarantees failure.
Moving forward guarantees growth.

Progress is Measured in Inches, Not Miles

You don't have to make massive leaps today.
You don't have to conquer mountains.
You just need to move an inch closer.

- Read one page.
- Make one call.
- Save one dollar.
- Write one paragraph.
- Practice one skill for ten minutes.

Tiny, unimpressive actions —
repeated daily —
build unstoppable momentum.
Consistency beats intensity.
It's not about sprinting for a week.
It's about stepping forward every single day.

The Lie of "Later"

Later is a lie.
"Later" is where dreams go to die.
"Later" is where regret grows like a disease.
There will never be a perfect day.
There will never be a moment when you are fully ready.
You don't need perfect.
You need progress.

Start messy.
Start scared.
Start uncertain.
    But **start today.**

You are Closer Than You Think

When you move,
you realize the dream isn't sitting across a desert.
It's waiting just a few brave steps away.
    Every time you choose action over fear,
you tear down the walls between you and your destiny.
    Every time you show up,
the impossible becomes inevitable.
    You are not lost.
You are not late.
You are not hopeless.
    You are simply one step away.
    Take it..

CHAPTER THREE

The Enemy Inside: Laziness and Fear

The biggest battles you will fight on your journey to success will not be against others.

They will be against yourself.

You will not be defeated by competitors.

You will be defeated by hesitation, excuses, fear, and laziness — if you let them.

The real enemy lives inside.

And unless you recognize it,

you will keep losing battles you don't even know you're fighting.

Laziness: The Silent Thief

Laziness rarely looks like laziness.
It disguises itself cleverly:

- "I'll do it tomorrow."
- "I'm not feeling motivated today."
- "I'm too tired; I deserve a break."
- "It's not the right time yet."
- "Let me first plan perfectly, then I'll act."

These sound harmless.
Even reasonable.
But behind every soft excuse,
there is a silent theft happening.
Every delayed action steals your future achievements.
Every skipped effort steals your future confidence.
Every postponed step pushes your dreams further away.
Laziness doesn't announce itself with alarms.
It whispers lullabies of comfort — until one day you wake up realizing years
have passed.
And worse than failure is **regret** —
the painful realization that you could have been so much more,
if only you had moved when it mattered.

Fear: The Invisible Wall

Fear will not always appear as trembling hands or sweaty palms.
Sometimes it appears as:

- Overthinking every small decision.
- Planning endlessly but never starting.
- Seeking everyone's approval before taking a step.
- Doubting your ability without even trying.

Fear is an invisible wall.
It's not real — but it feels solid when you stand still in front of it.
And the longer you stare at fear,
the bigger it grows in your mind.

But here's the secret:
Fear shrinks when you walk toward it.
When you take action despite being afraid,
you realize most fears were smoke, not walls.
Most fears were illusions magnified by your mind.

You Don't Need to Kill Fear — You Need to Move Anyway

The goal is not to become fearless.
The goal is to become brave.
Fear never fully disappears.
It walks with every dreamer, every doer, every builder.
But the successful ones don't wait for fear to leave.
They move forward even while fear whispers doubts in their ears.
Bravery is action despite fear.
Every time you act while scared,
you train your brain that **action is stronger than anxiety.**
Every time you move when lazy,
you prove to yourself that **discipline is stronger than desire for comfort.**

How to Fight Laziness and Fear:

- *Move immediately when you feel resistance.*

  (Don't negotiate with your brain. Just move.)

- *Set micro-goals.*

  (Not "write a book" — just "write 200 words today.")

- *Limit decision time.*

  (Set a timer: 10 minutes to decide, then act.)

- *Celebrate tiny wins.*

  (Every small action matters.)

- *Visualize the cost of inaction.*

(Ask yourself: "If I don't act today, what will it cost me a year from now?")

Action Kills Doubt

When you feel overwhelmed, act.
When you feel tired, act.
When you feel unworthy, act.
When you feel afraid, act.
Action does not guarantee success immediately.
But inaction guarantees failure permanently.
Your mind will always offer a thousand reasons to wait.
Your dreams only need one reason to begin:
You are worth it.

CHAPTER FOUR

Building the Muscle of Discipline

If success was based purely on talent, the world would be full of successful people.

If success was based only on intelligence, every academic genius would be a billionaire.

But success is not determined by talent or intelligence alone.

Success is built on discipline.

Discipline is the invisible engine behind every lasting achievement. It is the quiet, stubborn decision to show up, day after day, regardless of mood, motivation, or obstacles.

It is the refusal to quit on yourself.

It is the understanding that dreams are not wished into existence — they are built.

Motivation Is Temporary. Discipline Is Permanent.

Motivation is wonderful — when it's there.
It makes you feel invincible, passionate, excited.
But motivation is an emotion —
and like all emotions, it rises and falls.
You cannot rely on motivation to build your future.
Discipline is what carries you through when motivation disappears.
When you're tired.
When you're uninspired.
When you're doubting yourself.
When no one is watching.
Discipline is loyalty to your dreams,
even on the days you don't feel like dreaming.

Discipline Is a Muscle — and It Can Be Trained

No one is born disciplined.
Discipline is not a gift.
It's a skill — like running, playing the guitar, or cooking.
And like every skill,
it grows stronger with consistent training.
The first day you try to build discipline,
it will feel heavy.
You will fail.
You will want to quit.
But every time you resist the temptation to skip your work,
every time you show up even when it's hard,
every time you act instead of procrastinating,
you lift the weight.
And with every repetition, you grow stronger.
Discipline today builds freedom tomorrow.

How to Build Your Discipline Muscle:

- _Start small, but start daily._

(Tiny daily actions are better than heroic occasional efforts.)

- *Design your environment.*

  (Remove distractions; make good choices easier.)

- *Have a fixed time for important tasks.*

  (Same time every day builds automatic habits.)

- *Expect failure — but refuse surrender.*

  (Missing one day is human. Missing two is a pattern.)

- *Reward yourself after consistency.*

  (Celebrate streaks, no matter how small.)
Discipline is not about perfection.
It's about persistence.
  It's about winning more days than you lose.

<u>Discipline = Freedom</u>

The world teaches us that freedom means doing what you want, when you want.
  But real freedom is being able to do what you should do — even when you don't want to.
  When you build discipline:

- You control your time.
- You control your emotions.
- You control your future.

  Without discipline,
you are a slave to moods, distractions, and short-term pleasures.
  With discipline,
you are a master of your destiny.

Freedom is not given —
Freedom is earned through disciplined living.

Discipline Feels Heavy at First — Then It Feels Light

At first, discipline feels like a burden.
It feels like sacrifice.
    But over time,
discipline becomes lighter.
    It becomes your default.
Your normal.
Your secret weapon.
    The things that once seemed impossible become automatic.
    And then the results —
the confidence, the growth, the success —
become so sweet that you wonder why you ever resisted them.

Discipline Is Love

Discipline is not punishment.
    It is self-respect.
    It is love in action.
    When you discipline yourself to wake up early,
to study harder,
to practice longer,
to push deeper,
you are telling your future self:

> *"I care about you.
> I believe in you.
> I am fighting for you."*

And there is no greater love than that.

CHAPTER FIVE

Failing Forward

Failure is not the opposite of success.
Failure is the path to success.

Every person who has ever achieved anything extraordinary has failed — not once, but many, many times.

The difference is not that successful people avoid failure. It's that they fail forward.

They fall — but they fall in the direction of their dreams. They stumble — but they stumble toward growth.

Failure is Feedback

Failure is not a verdict.
It's information.

Every time you fail, you learn:

- What doesn't work.
- What needs improvement.
- What skills must be sharpened.
- What mindsets must be changed.

Failure gives you data that success never will.
If you're smart,
you don't just suffer failure — you **study** it.
You don't just endure it — you **extract lessons** from it.
Failure is feedback —
and feedback is fuel.

Winners Lose More Than Losers

Strange but true:

- The best athletes have lost more games than amateurs have played.
- The best entrepreneurs have launched more failed businesses than most people dream of.
- The best writers have been rejected more times than average people submit.

Success is not the absence of failure.
Success is surviving enough failures to get to your breakthrough.
The problem isn't failing.
The problem is **quitting after failure**.

The Fear of Failure is Worse Than Failure Itself

Most people are not stopped by failure.
They are stopped by the fear of failure.
They never apply.
They never attempt.
They never risk.
They never reach.

Because they imagine the embarrassment, the rejection, the disappointment.

But when you actually fail —
you realize it's not fatal.

You're still breathing.
You're still standing.
You're still capable.

The fear was worse than the event.

Once you taste failure and survive it,
you become fearless.

You understand that failure is not a dead-end.
It's just a detour.

Failing Forward Means Three Things:

1. *You Learn Fast*
You don't hide from failure — you analyze it.
You ask, "What went wrong? What can I improve?"

2. *You Adjust Fast*
You tweak your approach.
You change strategies, not dreams.

3. *You Move Fast*
You don't sit in self-pity.
You act again while the lesson is still fresh.

Successful people fail often —
but they fail forward so quickly that from the outside, it looks like smooth success.

It's not smooth.
It's a series of corrected failures.

Fall Seven Times, Stand Up Eight

Japanese Proverb:

"Fall seven times, stand up eight."

This is the spirit of failing forward.

Not every step will be glorious.
Not every attempt will win.
Not every effort will shine.
But every time you fall and rise again,
you are one step closer to your goal.
Fall — but fall forward.
Fail — but fail with momentum.
And you will reach places that perfect people who never risk anything
will never see.

Failure is Temporary. Growth is Permanent.

Every failure is a temporary sting.
A lesson.
A season.
But every lesson, every scar, every hard-won insight —
stays with you forever.
Growth compounds.
Wisdom accumulates.
And when you succeed —
(and you will) —
you will realize that every painful fall was worth it.
Because it didn't destroy you —
it built you.

CHAPTER SIX

Protecting the Dream

Dreams are fragile in the beginning.

They are like tiny flames in a world full of storms.

They can be easily blown out by doubt, fear, negativity, and even well-meaning people.

If you are serious about building the life you want,

you must learn this early:

Your first responsibility is not to prove your dream.

Your first responsibility is to protect your dream.

<u>Not Everyone Will Understand</u>

Don't expect everyone to clap when you start chasing your dreams.

Don't expect applause, encouragement, or even understanding.

Most people see the world not as it is, but as they are.

Their fears, failures, and limitations shape what they believe is possible —

not just for themselves, but for you too.
When you tell them your big dream:

- Some will laugh.
- Some will advise you to "be realistic."
- Some will ignore you completely.
- Some will secretly envy your courage.

Understand:
Their reaction has nothing to do with your potential.
It only reveals their own mindset.
Protect your dream from their doubts.
Protect it like you would protect a newborn baby —
carefully, fiercely, lovingly.

Protecting Your Dream Means Limiting Exposure

In the early stages,
your dream needs nurturing — not criticism.
That means:

- Share it selectively.
- Keep it private until it's strong enough to withstand public attack.
- Avoid over-explaining to people who aren't qualified to advise you.

You don't owe everyone an explanation.
You owe your dream a safe place to grow.

Build a Fence Around Your Mind

Your mind is the soil where your dream is planted.
If you allow toxic thoughts, doubts, and negativity to flood it,
your dream will wither.
Protect your mind by:

- Choosing what you read, watch, and listen to.
- Surrounding yourself with positive, ambitious voices.
- Limiting conversations that drain your energy or belittle your ambition.

- Affirming your belief daily: *"My dream is valid. My dream is worth fighting for."*

You cannot plant seeds of greatness while watering weeds of fear.

Protecting Doesn't Mean Hiding Forever

Protecting your dream doesn't mean hiding in fear forever.
  There will come a time to speak boldly.
To act publicly.
To defend your vision without shame.
  But timing matters.
  You don't expose a seed to storms;
you expose a tree — after it has roots deep enough to survive.
  Similarly,
build your dream in private —
until it's strong enough to live in public.

Your Dream is Sacred

You must treat your dream as sacred —
because it is.
  It's not "just an idea."
It's a calling.
A responsibility.
A gift planted in your heart for a reason.
  Maybe the world doesn't see it yet.
That's okay.
They're not supposed to.
  You are the guardian of your dream.
  Until the world is ready to believe —
you must believe enough for everyone.

The World Will Try to Shrink You

As you walk forward,
the world will try to make you smaller:

- "Who do you think you are?"
- "It's too hard."
- "It's too late."
- "Be realistic."

Smile politely.
Ignore them ruthlessly.
You are not here to live someone else's limits.
You are here to explore the full size of your soul.
You are here to stretch the boundaries of what's possible.
You are here to honor the dream given to you — not by society, not by critics,
but by the voice deep inside that knows what you are truly capable of.

Protect First. Build Second. Then Inspire.

First, protect the dream.
Second, build it quietly, daily.
Third, when the time comes — inspire others by living it out loud.
Your life will become proof that protecting your dream was worth it.
You won't have to convince anyone.
Your results will speak.
Your journey will shine.
Your dream will roar.
And you will smile —
knowing you protected something priceless
until it could protect itself.

CHAPTER SEVEN

The Day It Will Happen

There will come a day —
an ordinary day —
when everything changes.
It won't be announced.
There won't be trumpets, banners, or warning signs.
It might start like any other day:
A messy morning.
A bad mood.
A cloudy sky.
But then, something you planted long ago —
a seed of discipline, belief, courage —
will break through the surface.

The world will see in a moment
what you built quietly for years.

It Happens in Silence First

Breakthroughs don't happen because of one grand event.
They happen because of countless unseen efforts:

- The mornings you woke up early when no one noticed.
- The nights you worked after everyone slept.
- The battles you fought inside yourself and won silently.
- The days you showed up even when it felt pointless.

The harvest happens in public,
but the planting, watering, and weeding happens in private.

Success Feels Invisible — Until It Doesn't

Most of success feels boring:

- Showing up again.
- Pushing a little further.
- Fixing one more small mistake.
- Practicing when no one cares.
- It feels like nothing is changing.

It feels like the dream is mocking you.
But change is happening beneath the surface,
where you cannot yet see.
Just like bamboo grows roots for five years underground
before it shoots up 90 feet in five weeks,
your dream is preparing for its breakout moment.
Trust the roots.

You Won't Recognize It at First

The day your dream starts breaking through,
you might not even realize it immediately.
It may look like:

- A small opportunity.
- A chance meeting.
- An unexpected call.
- A new burst of confidence.

Success rarely knocks loudly.
It taps quietly,
offering you a chance to step into the next level.
If you have been faithful with your small steps,
you will recognize the tap.
And you will answer it boldly.

Your Preparation Determines Your Celebration

The day your breakthrough comes,
you won't rise to the level of your dreams.
You will fall to the level of your preparation.
If you have trained yourself in discipline, resilience, patience —
you will be ready.
You will not panic.
You will not fumble.
You will rise because you have practiced rising
long before anyone was watching.

Not "If," But "When"

If you stay consistent,
the question is never if it will happen.
The only question is when.

- When will your effort collide with opportunity?
- When will your preparation meet the right moment?
- When will your belief overpower your doubts?

Stay the course.
The day is already on its way toward you,
even if you can't see it yet.

Imagine the Moment Now

Imagine it:
    The moment you realize it was all worth it.
The moment you step onto the stage, or sign the deal, or publish the book,
or open the business, or reach the dream you once feared was impossible.
    The moment you look back and realize:

- Every small step mattered.
- Every silent effort was seen.
- Every lonely battle was not in vain.

    That day will come.
    And when it does,
you will know deeply, without doubt:
    You were never too far.
You were only one step away.

CHAPTER EIGHT

You Are Not Alone

Dream chasing can feel lonely.
You might believe you're the only one struggling.
The only one doubting.
The only one facing rejection after rejection.
But here's the truth:
You are not alone.
Every great journey feels isolating at some point.
But that isolation is an illusion.
You are walking a path walked by thousands before you —
and thousands walking beside you right now, even if you cannot see them.

The Silent Army of Dreamers

Every day, around the world, millions of people are quietly:

- Waking up early to build something no one understands yet.
- Staying up late to study after exhausting day jobs.
- Practicing skills alone while others are partying.
- Fighting self-doubt, fear, fatigue — and still moving forward.

They are not famous.
They are not celebrated — yet.
They are invisible warriors, building futures piece by piece.
You are one of them.
You belong to a silent army of people who refuse to settle.

Even the Greatest Felt Alone

Think of anyone you admire:

- Entrepreneurs like Steve Jobs.
- Athletes like Serena Williams.
- Writers like J.K. Rowling.
- Leaders like Dr. A.P.J. Abdul Kalam.

Every single one of them went through seasons where they felt misunderstood, isolated, unsupported.
When Steve Jobs was fired from Apple, he felt abandoned.
When J.K. Rowling was rejected by multiple publishers, she questioned her worth.
When Kalam missed key opportunities, he wrestled with self-doubt.
They all walked through loneliness —
and so will you.
But they kept walking.
And eventually, the world caught up.

Loneliness Is a Test — and a Teacher

Feeling alone tests your commitment:

- Will you continue even when no one claps?
- Will you believe even when no one validates you?
- Will you persist even when no one watches?

If you do, you build something priceless:
Self-reliance.
The ability to motivate yourself internally.
The strength to keep moving based on vision, not applause.
Loneliness teaches you to trust your inner compass —
not external noise.

Seek Your Tribe

While loneliness is a part of the journey,
you don't have to stay isolated forever.
There are people who will understand you:

- Fellow dreamers.
- Builders.
- Believers.

Seek them out:

- Join communities aligned with your goals.
- Read books written by those who walked ahead.
- Follow inspiring voices who lift your spirit.

Your tribe exists —
people who get it, who live it, who walk the same path.
Find them.
Support them.
Let them support you.
Together, the journey becomes lighter.

Invisible Hands Are Helping You

Sometimes help comes silently:

- A book that finds you at the right time.
- A stranger's encouraging words.
- A teacher who believes in you before you believe in yourself.

The universe often sends support,
even if it's not loud or obvious.
Stay open.
Stay receptive.
Stay grateful.
You are not walking alone —
even when it feels like it.

You Are Seen. You Are Supported.

Every step you take is seen —
even if not by the world yet.
Every sacrifice you make is sacred.
Every effort you pour in matters.
You are part of something bigger:
The brave, quiet movement of dreamers refusing to live small lives.
You are not foolish.
You are not wrong.
You are not invisible.
You are seen.
You are supported.
You are walking the right path.
And soon — very soon —
the world will recognize what you have always known:
You were never truly alone.
You were simply ahead.

CHAPTER NINE

The Journey Within

The world teaches us to chase things:

- Success.
- Money.
- Fame.
- Approval.

But the greatest journey you will ever take
is not across countries or through companies.
It is the journey within.
Because no matter how much you achieve outside,
if you lose yourself inside,
you have lost everything.

Success Without Self-Understanding Is Empty

You can have the best job, the biggest house, the highest salary —
and still feel hollow.
Why?
Because external success cannot fill internal emptiness.
True fulfillment comes from:

- Knowing who you are.
- Living aligned with your deepest values.
- Building a life that reflects your soul, not just your resume.

The real dream is not just to "make it" —
it's to make it while staying true to yourself.

The Inner World Shapes the Outer World

Your thoughts, beliefs, and emotions create your external reality.

- If you think you are worthy, you pursue opportunities.
- If you believe you are capable, you persist through obstacles.
- If you manage your emotions, you navigate challenges calmly.

Change inside, and the outside must follow.
Growth inside creates growth outside.
This is why some people with less "talent" succeed wildly —
because they win the inner game first.

Questions to Ask Yourself on the Journey Within:

- What do I truly want — beyond money or titles?
- What am I willing to suffer for?
- What values will I never compromise, even for success?
- Am I living according to my purpose, or according to others'
  expectations?
- When I am old, what kind of life story do I want to tell myself?

These questions are not easy.
They are uncomfortable.
But they are necessary.
  Without them, you risk building a life that looks impressive — but feels empty.

Self-Discovery Is a Lifelong Journey

You don't "find yourself" once and then stop.
  Every season of life demands deeper self-awareness.

- What energized you at 18 might not fulfill you at 28.
- What scared you at 25 might become your mission at 35.
- What you value today might evolve tomorrow.

  Stay curious about yourself.
  Keep asking, exploring, adjusting.
  Grow not just outward, but inward.

Inner Peace is a Superpower

In a noisy world chasing validation,
inner peace becomes a rare, magnetic force.

- When you are at peace, you make better decisions.
- When you are at peace, you are not desperate for approval.
- When you are at peace, you become unshakable.

  And inner peace comes from alignment:
  Living a life that matches your soul —
not the expectations forced on you.
  Chasing dreams that nourish your spirit —
not just impress your neighbors.

Success Is Not a Place — It's a State of Being

You don't reach success when you hit a number.
  You reach success when:

- You respect yourself.
- You trust yourself.
- You love the life you are building.
- You look in the mirror and are proud of who you are becoming.

   This is the real trophy.
This is the real treasure.
   And it can only be won
on the journey within.

CHAPTER TEN

One Step Beyond

All your life, you were told to wait.

Wait for the right time.

Wait for more experience.

Wait for permission.

Wait until you feel ready.

But now you know the truth:

The next step was always yours to take.

And once you take that step —

once you cross the invisible line between "dreaming" and "doing" —

a new world opens.
    You realize:
    You were never stuck.
You were never incapable.
You were never too late.
    You were simply one decision,
one action,
one belief away
from a completely different life.

The Step Most People Never Take

Most people live their whole lives standing at the edge.

- They dream loudly, but move quietly — backward.
- They plan for years, but act for days.
- They watch others build, while convincing themselves they could too...
  "someday."

    Don't live at the edge.
Don't settle for almost.
Don't become a fan of life when you were meant to be a player.
    The world does not belong to the most talented.
It belongs to the ones who step.

Stepping Beyond Means Accepting Discomfort

Growth lives outside the comfort zone.
    When you take that step beyond:

- You will feel fear.
- You will face criticism.
- You will make mistakes.
- You will question yourself.

    But you will also:

- Discover strengths you didn't know you had.

- Meet people who inspire you to level up.
- Build resilience that protects you in every storm.
- Experience victories you once thought belonged only to "special" people.

Discomfort is not a sign you are wrong.
It's a sign you are moving beyond your old limits.

One Step Changes Everything

History is not shaped by giant leaps.
It's shaped by individuals who dared to take one small, courageous step forward:

- The step to apply.
- The step to stand up.
- The step to speak out.
- The step to try again.

And after the first step?
Momentum.
Confidence.
New paths opening.
New you emerging.
The first step always looks small.
But in reality, it is massive —
because it separates those who dream from those who do.

You Already Have Everything You Need

You don't need more motivation.
You don't need more certificates.
You don't need more approval.
You already have:

- Enough courage to start.
- Enough wisdom to adjust.
- Enough resilience to endure.
- Enough passion to rise.

You are ready now.
You were ready yesterday.
You will be even more ready tomorrow.
But readiness is not a feeling.
It is a choice.
And today,
you can choose.

<u>*The World is Waiting for You*</u>

There are people you are meant to impact.
Lives you are meant to touch.
Dreams you are meant to fulfill.
    But none of that happens
until you step.
    One step beyond fear.
One step beyond doubt.
One step beyond hesitation.
    Step into the life that has been waiting for you
as long as you have been waiting for it.
    The first step changes you.
The next steps change the world.

You Are Not Just One Step Away Anymore — You Are One Step Beyond.

www.ingramcontent.com/pod-product-compliance
Lightning Source LLC
Chambersburg PA
CBHW020512160726
47991CB00007B/2919